For upcoming books and more, visit my website!

http://www.JosieCluney.com

You can find the 'Mystic Art' series on Facebook at

https://www.facebook.com/MysticArtBooks/

Stay updated and informed of any new releases coming out for your enjoyment!

'Legends of the Deep' is the first book in the 'Mystic Art' Adult Coloring in Books. All of the 25 beautifully designed images are hand drawn and produced for your enjoyment.
I hope you enjoy coloring in these Mystic Legends of the Deep, and find relaxation in their designs.

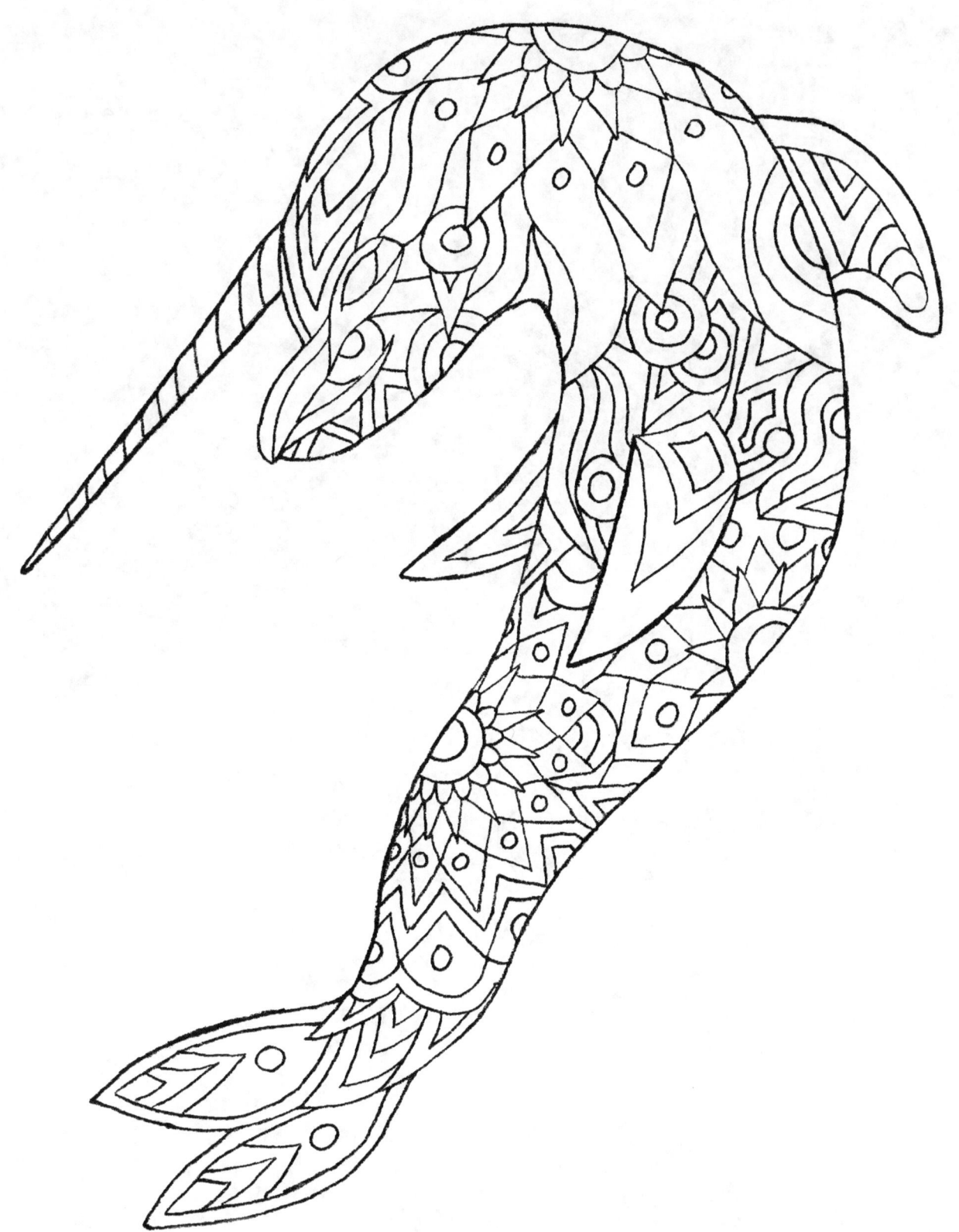

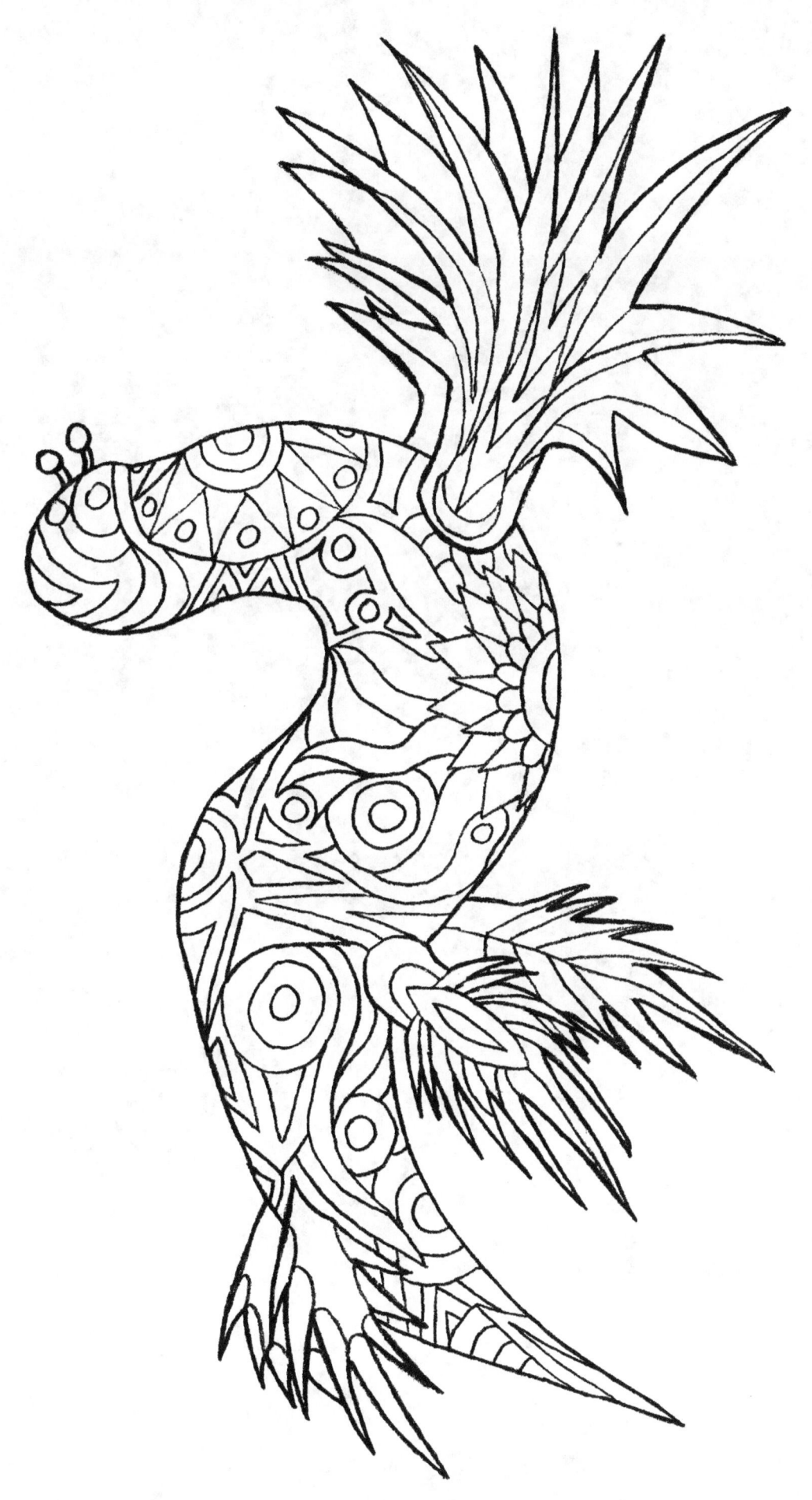

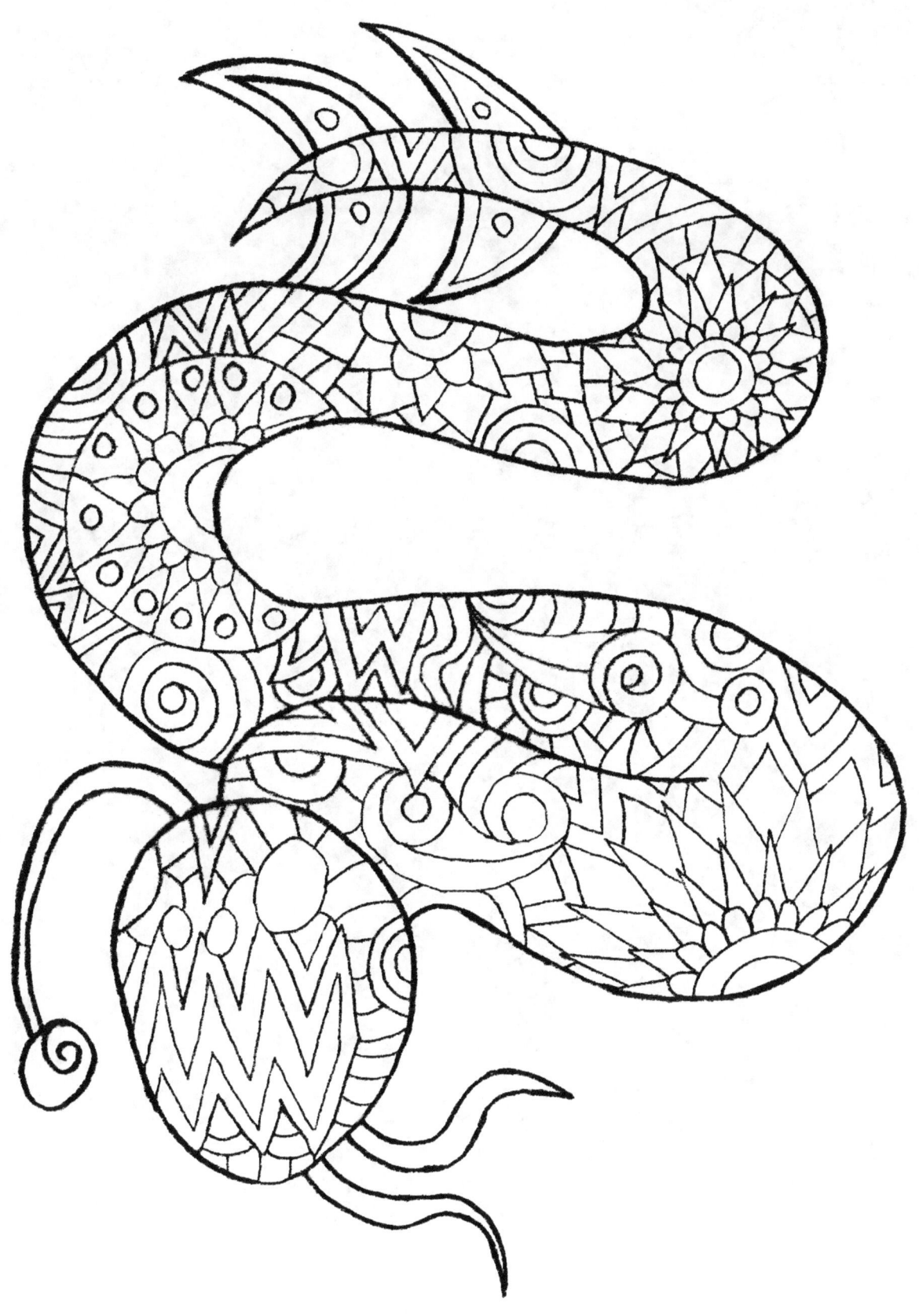

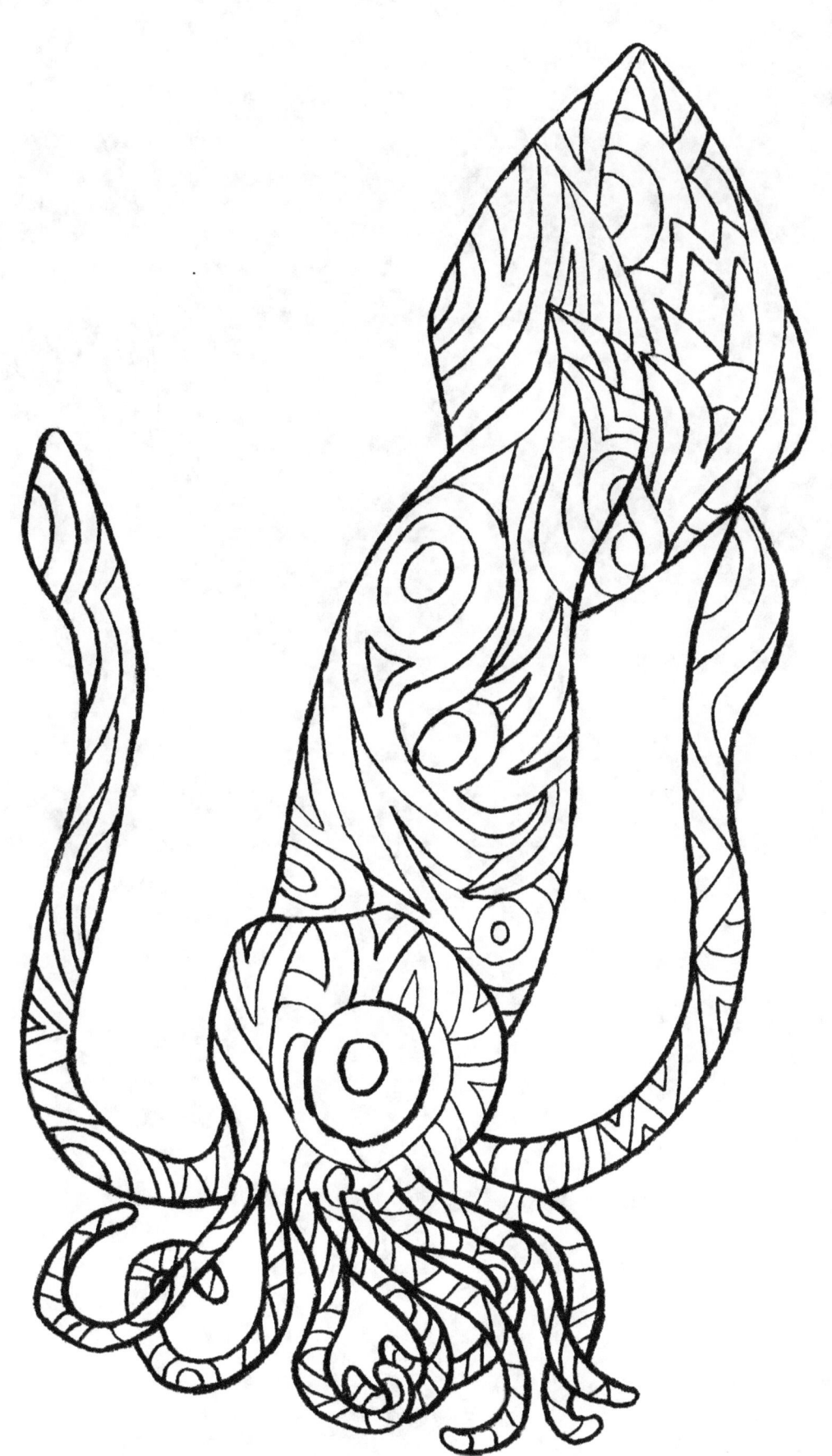

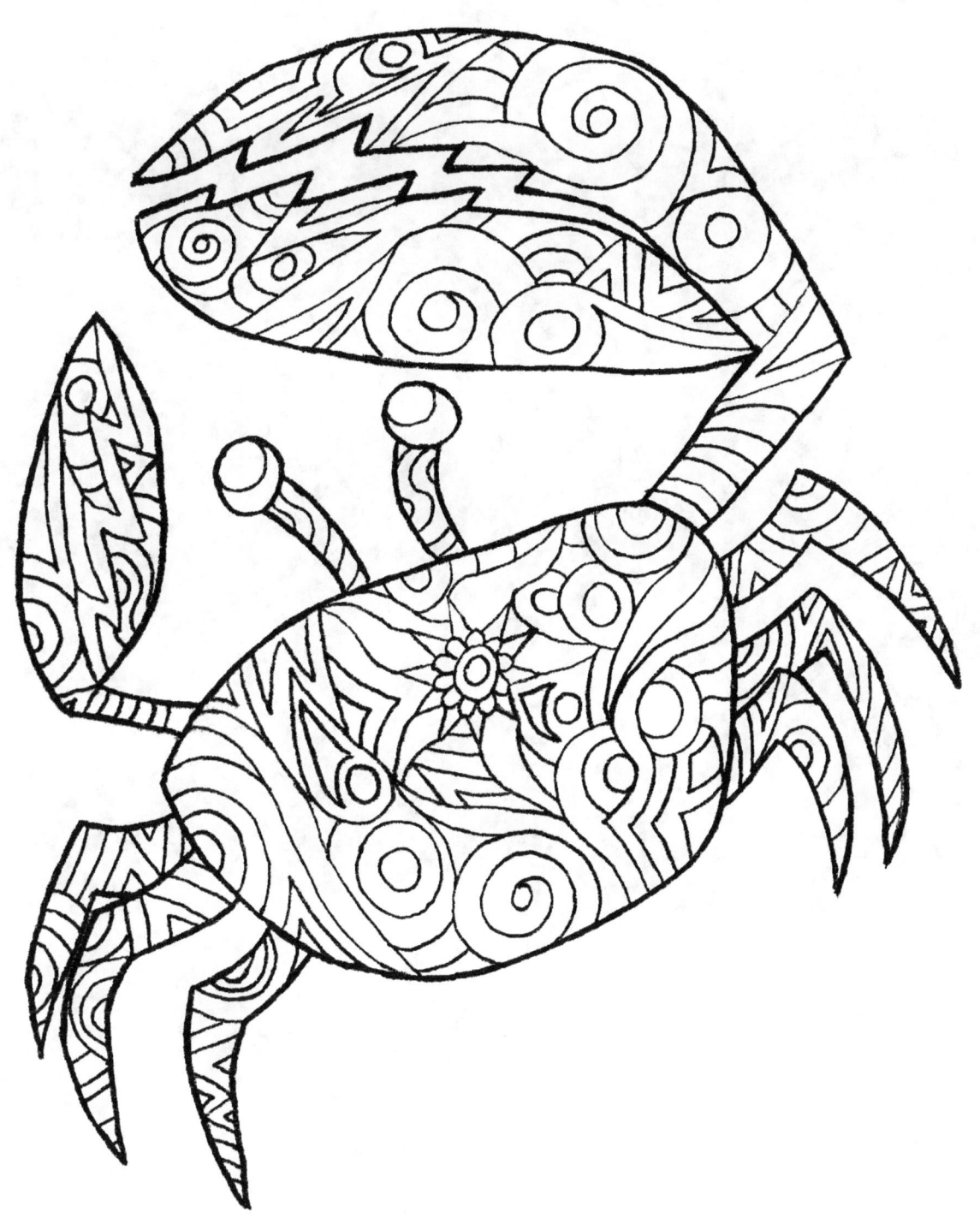

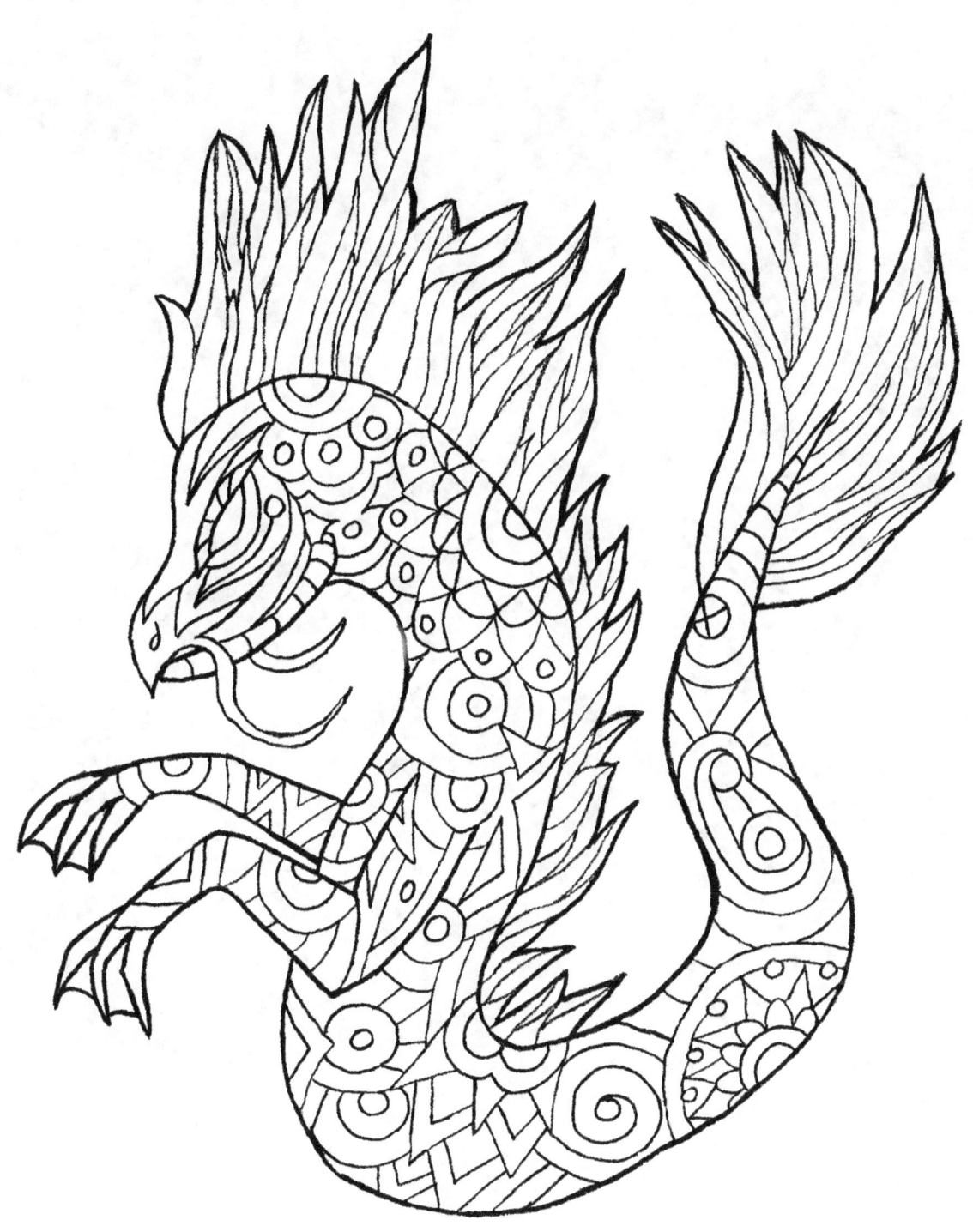

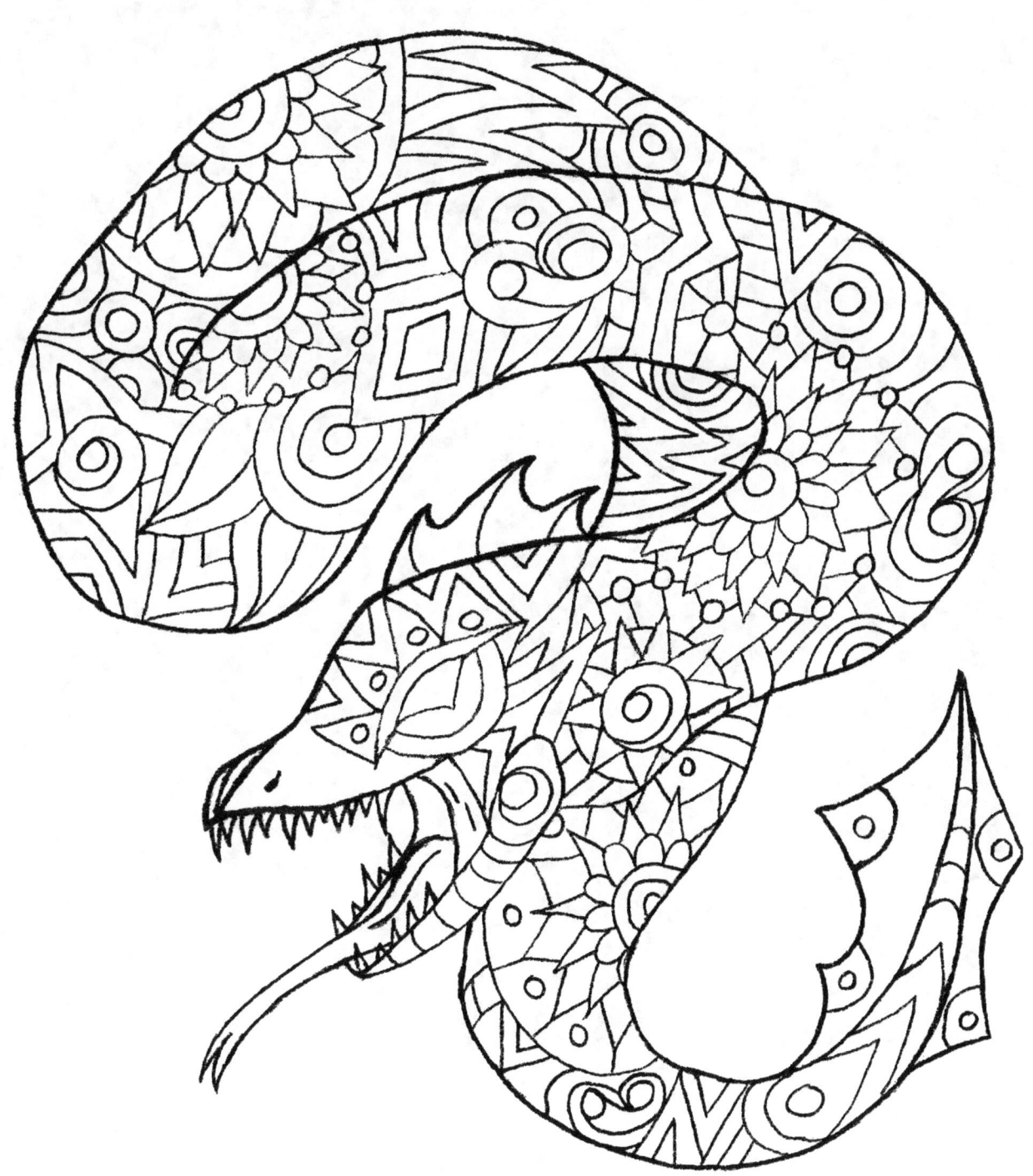

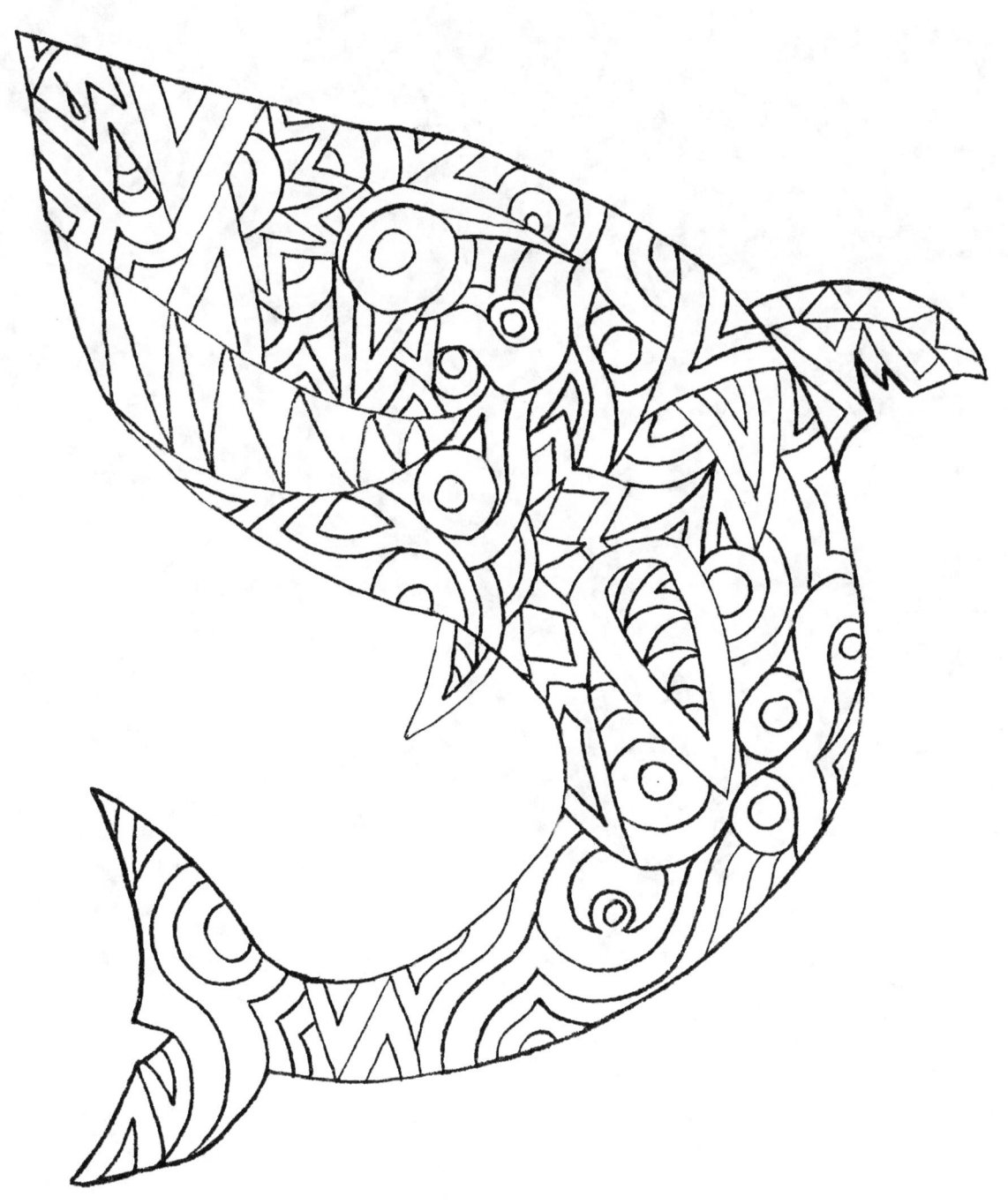

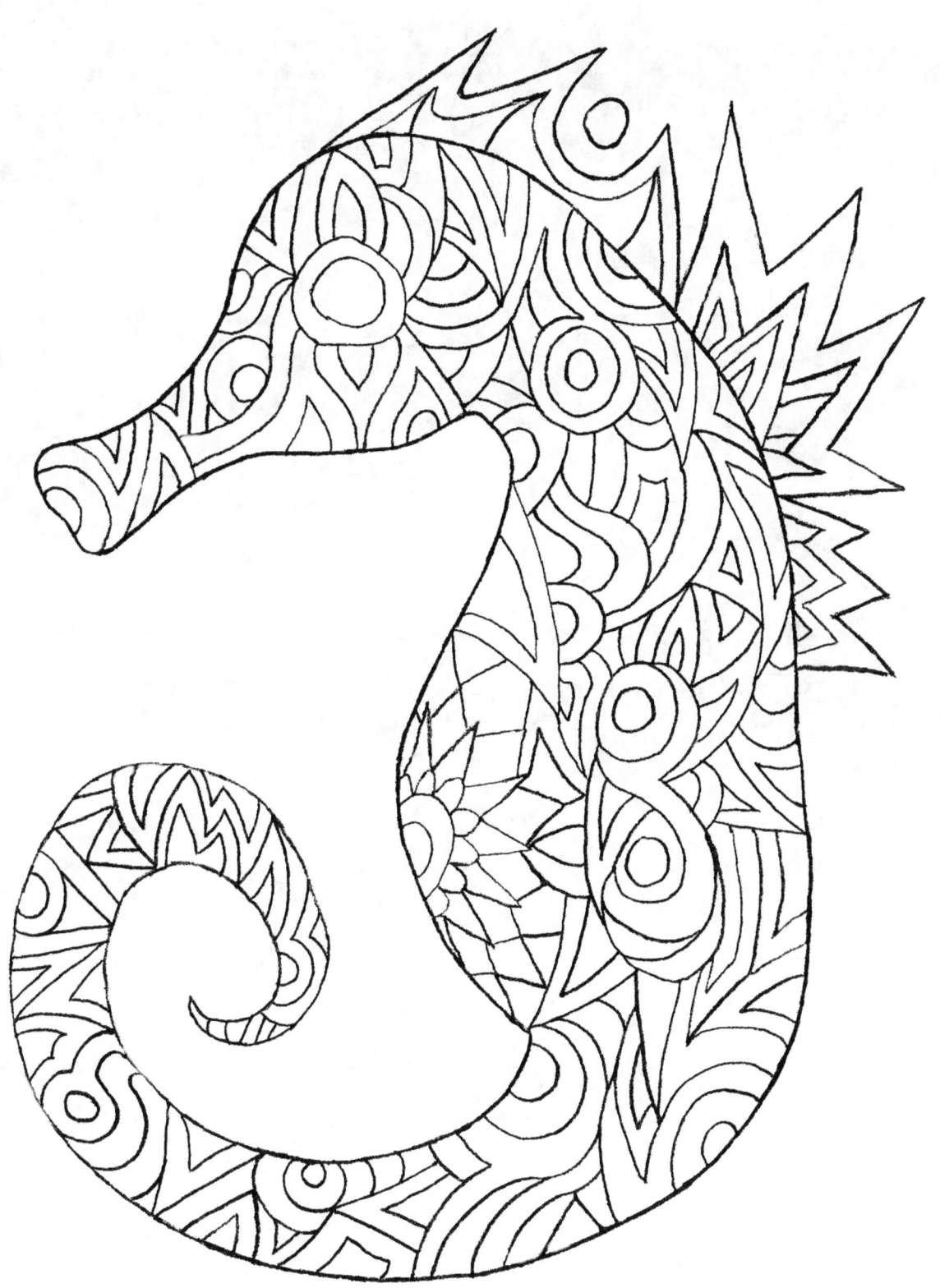

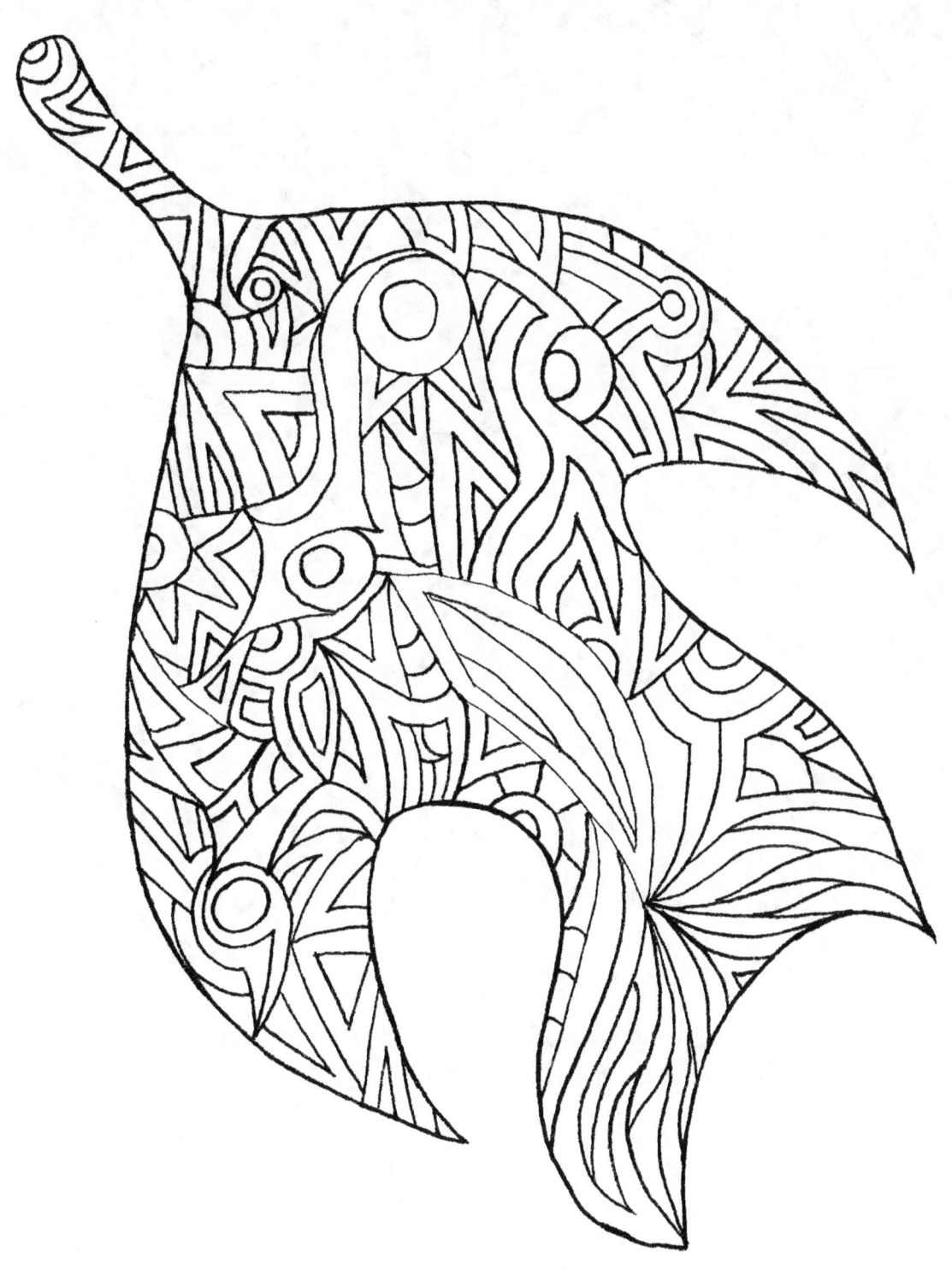

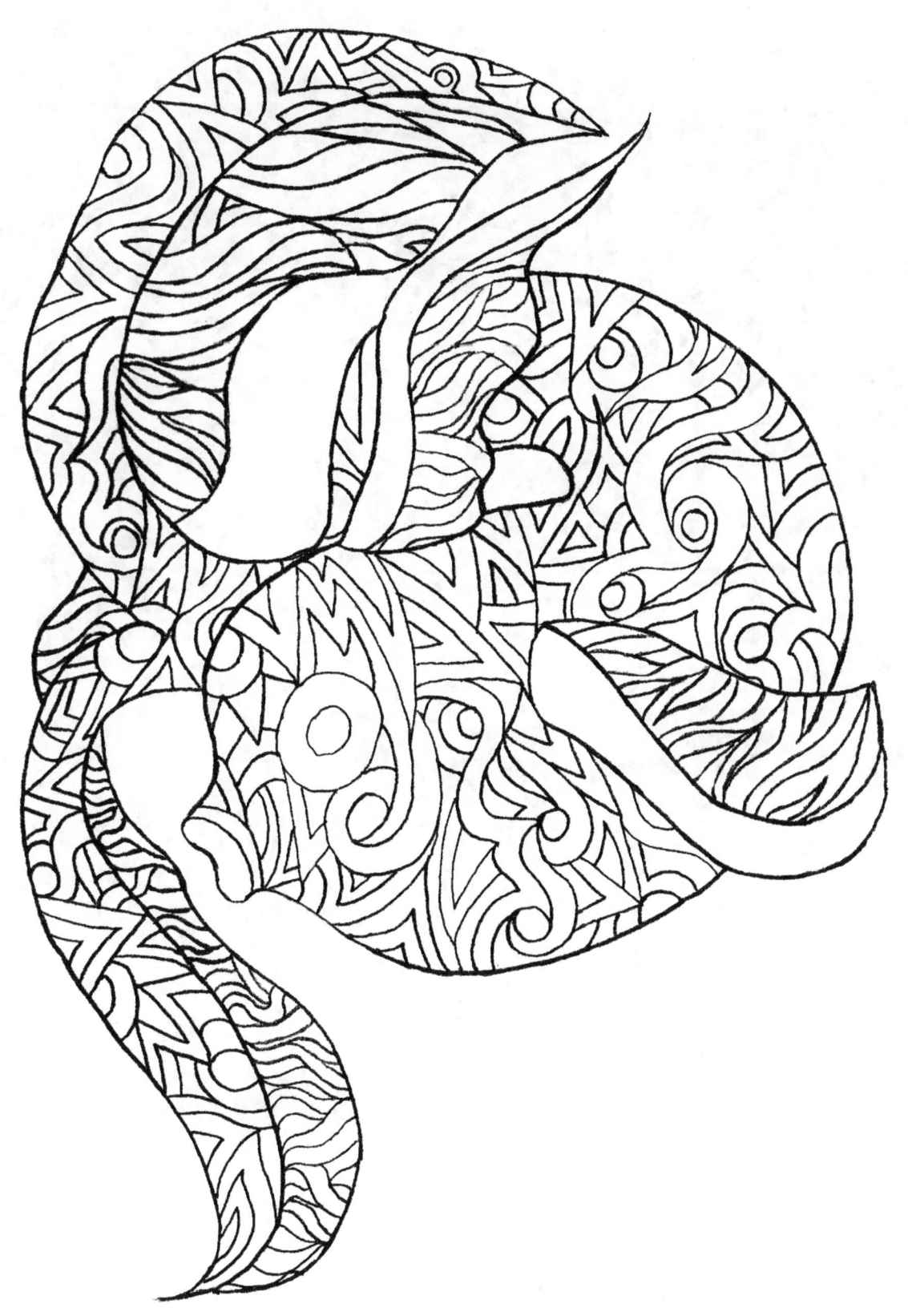

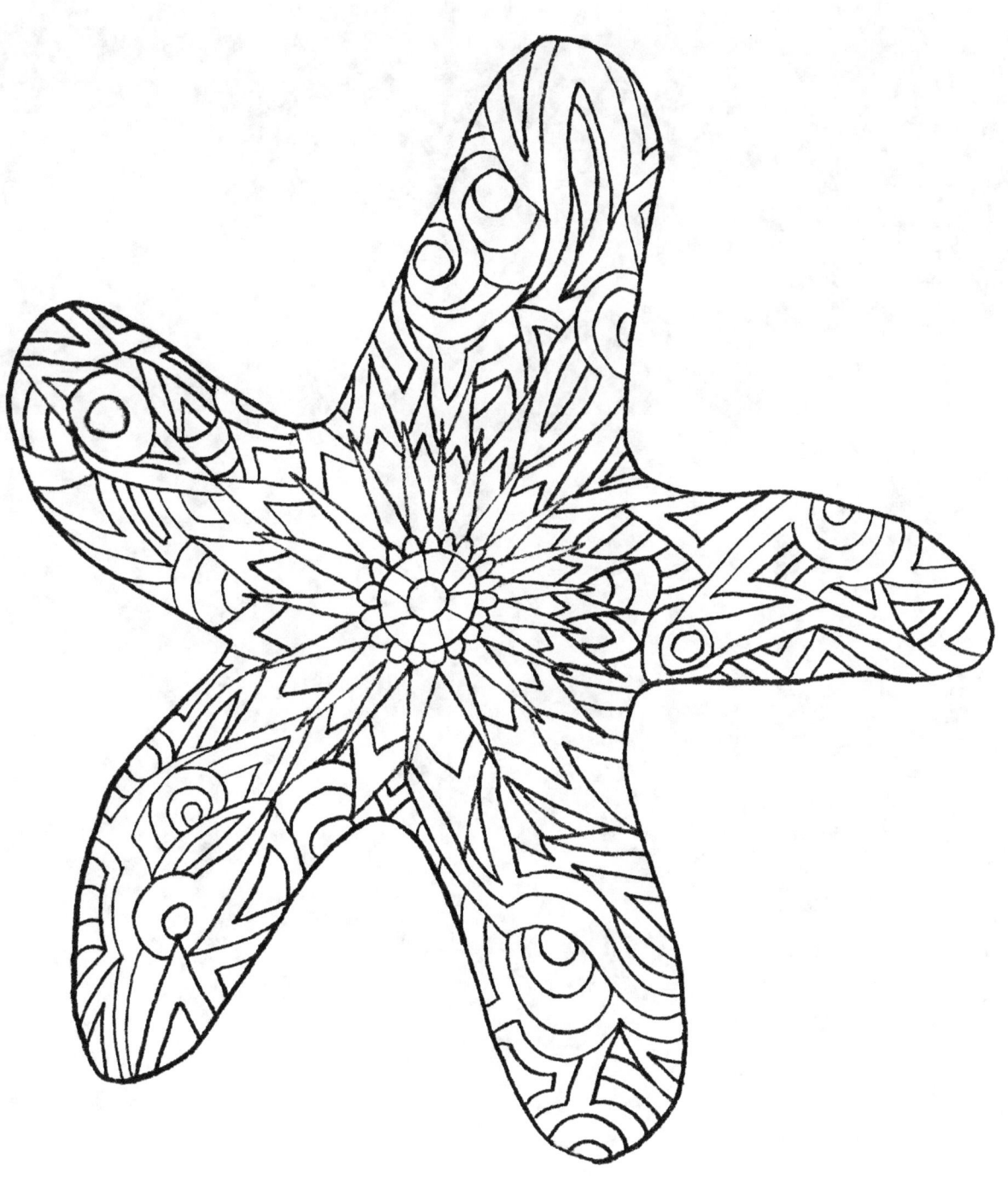

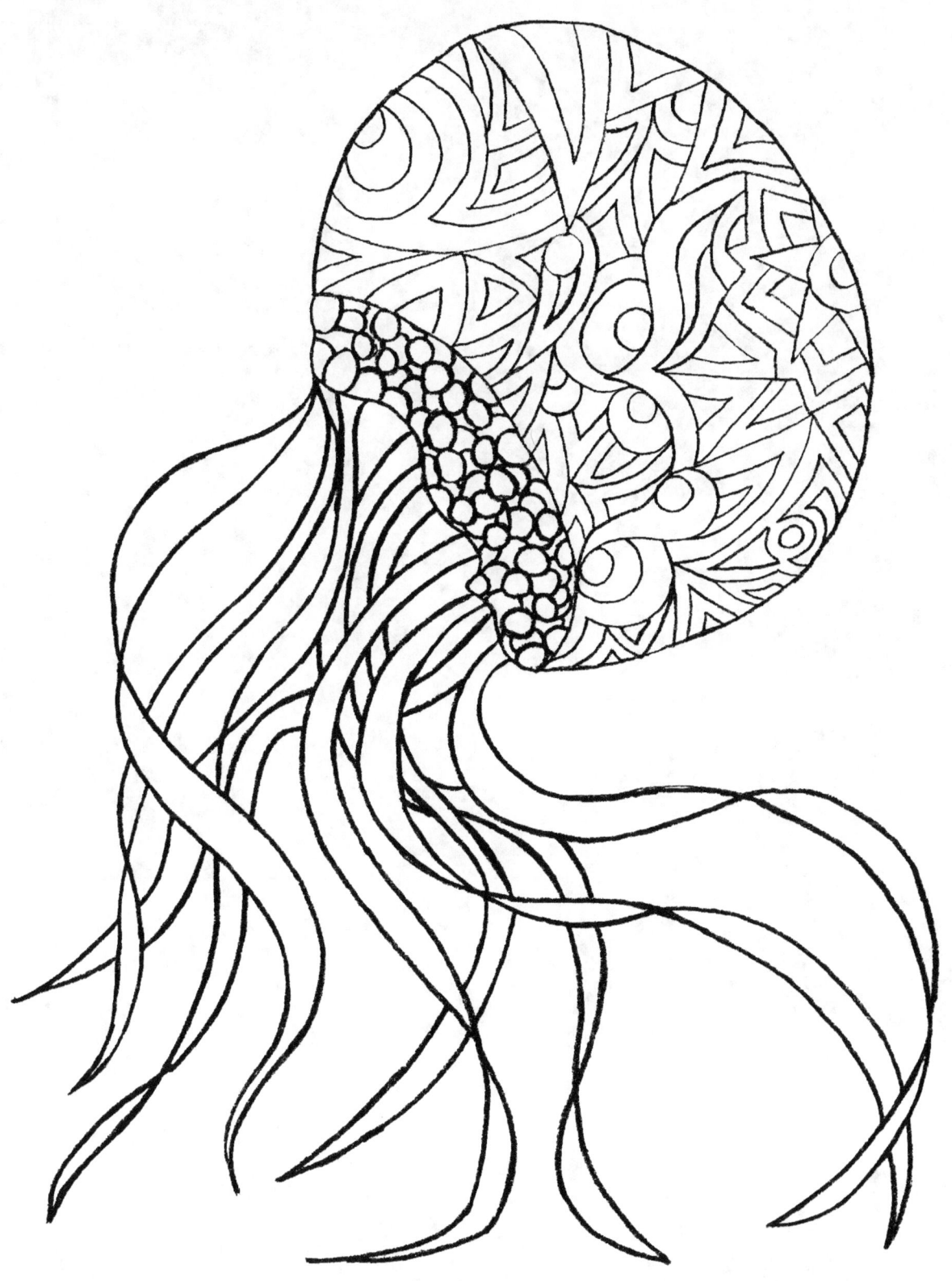

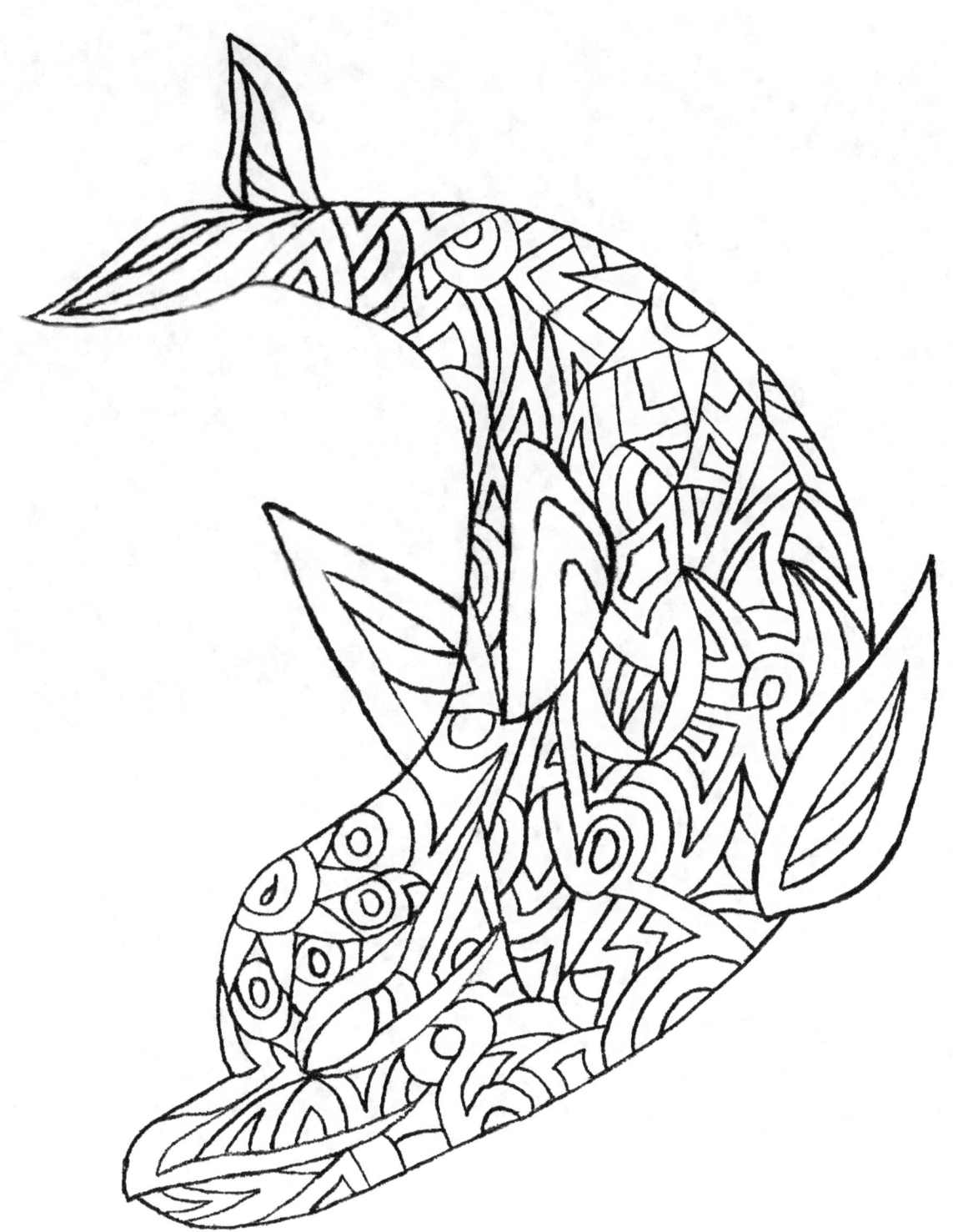

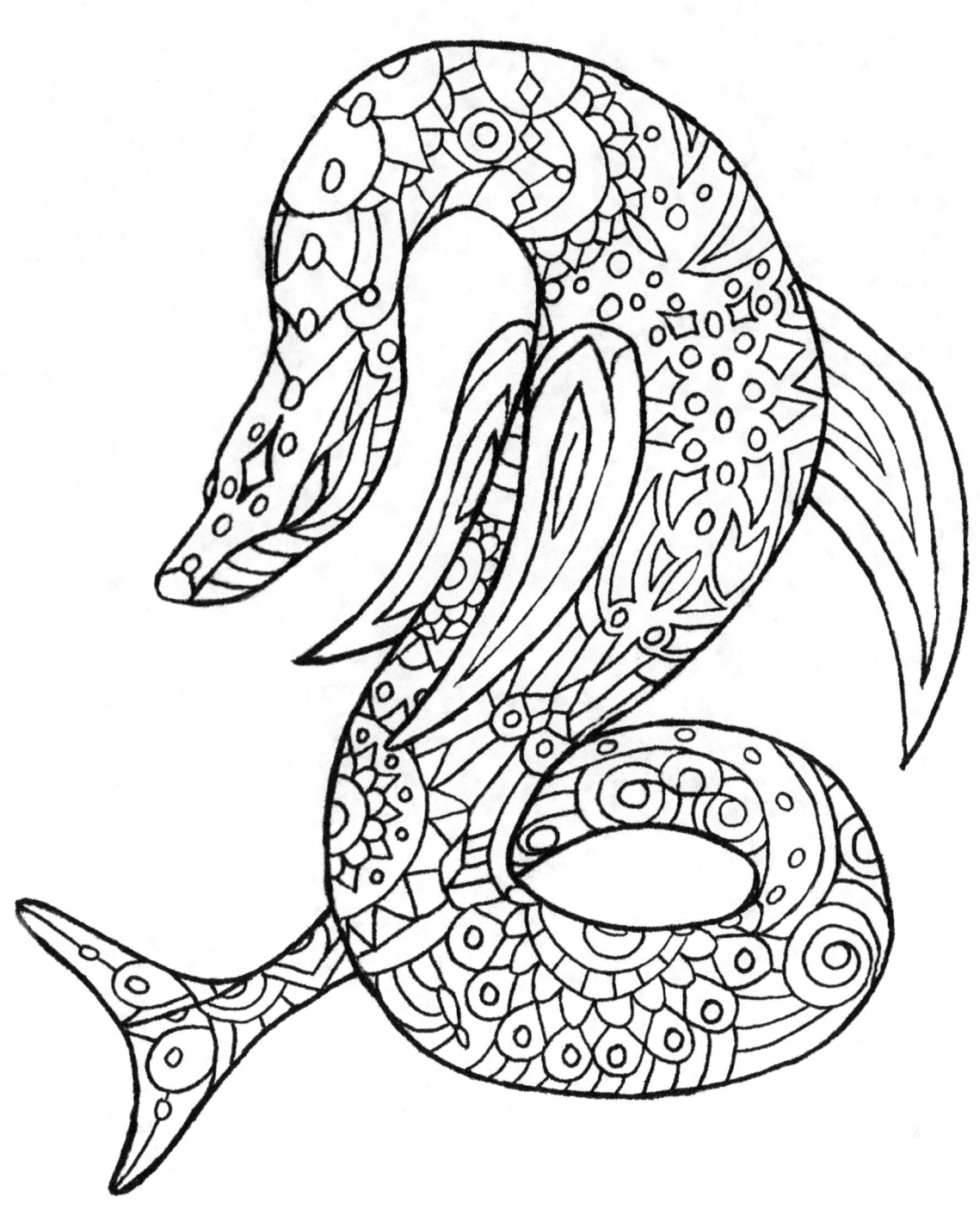

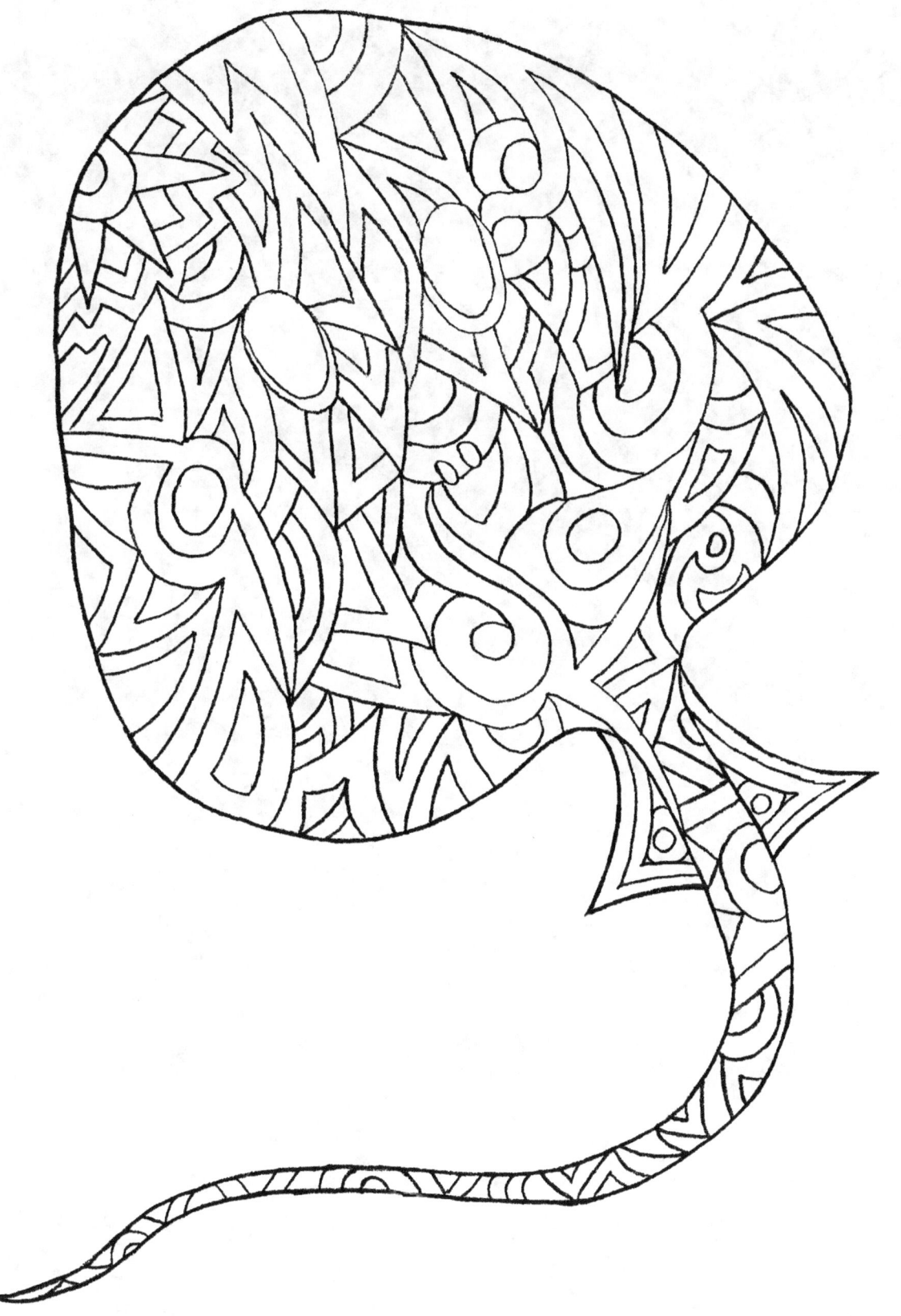

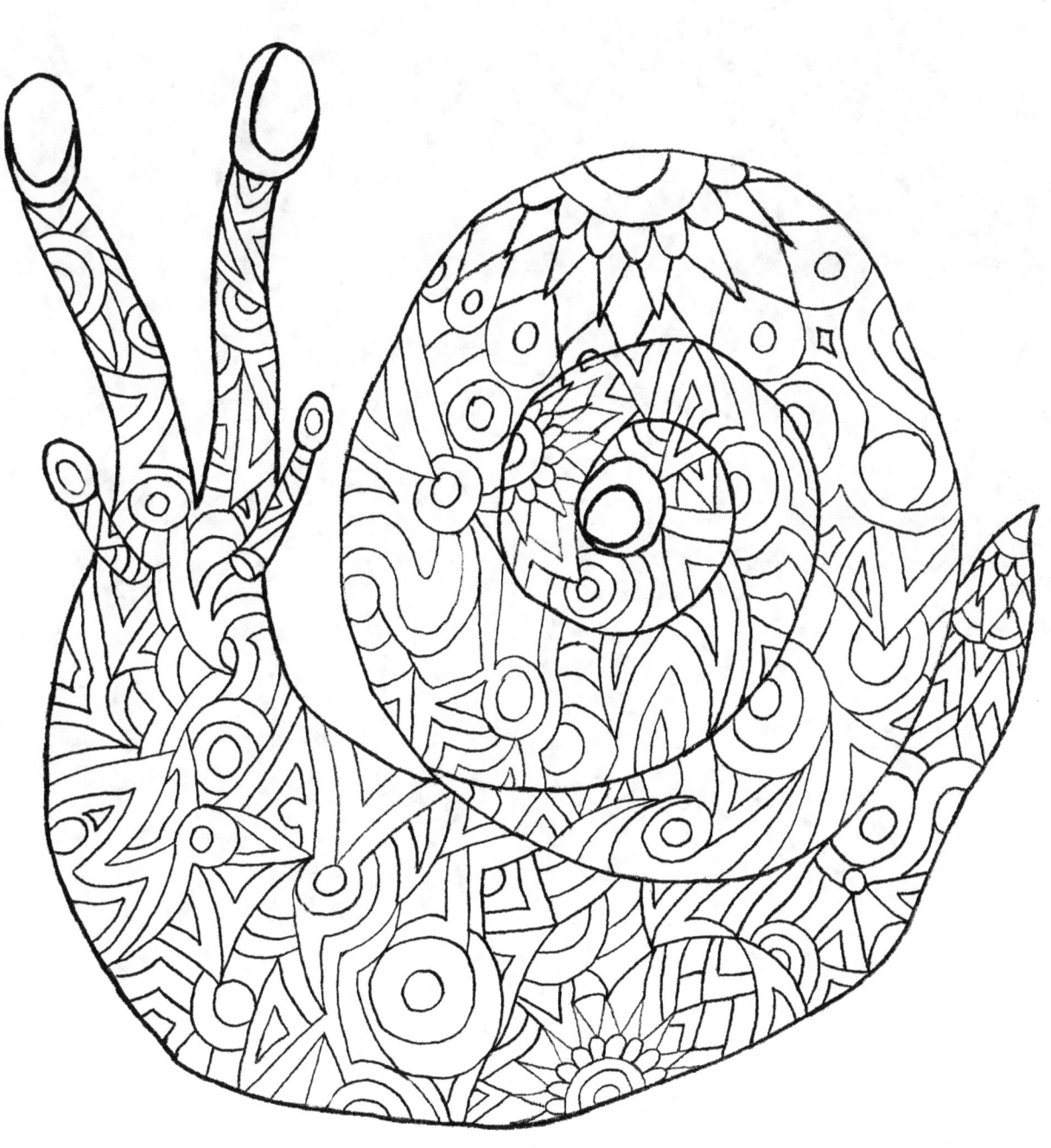

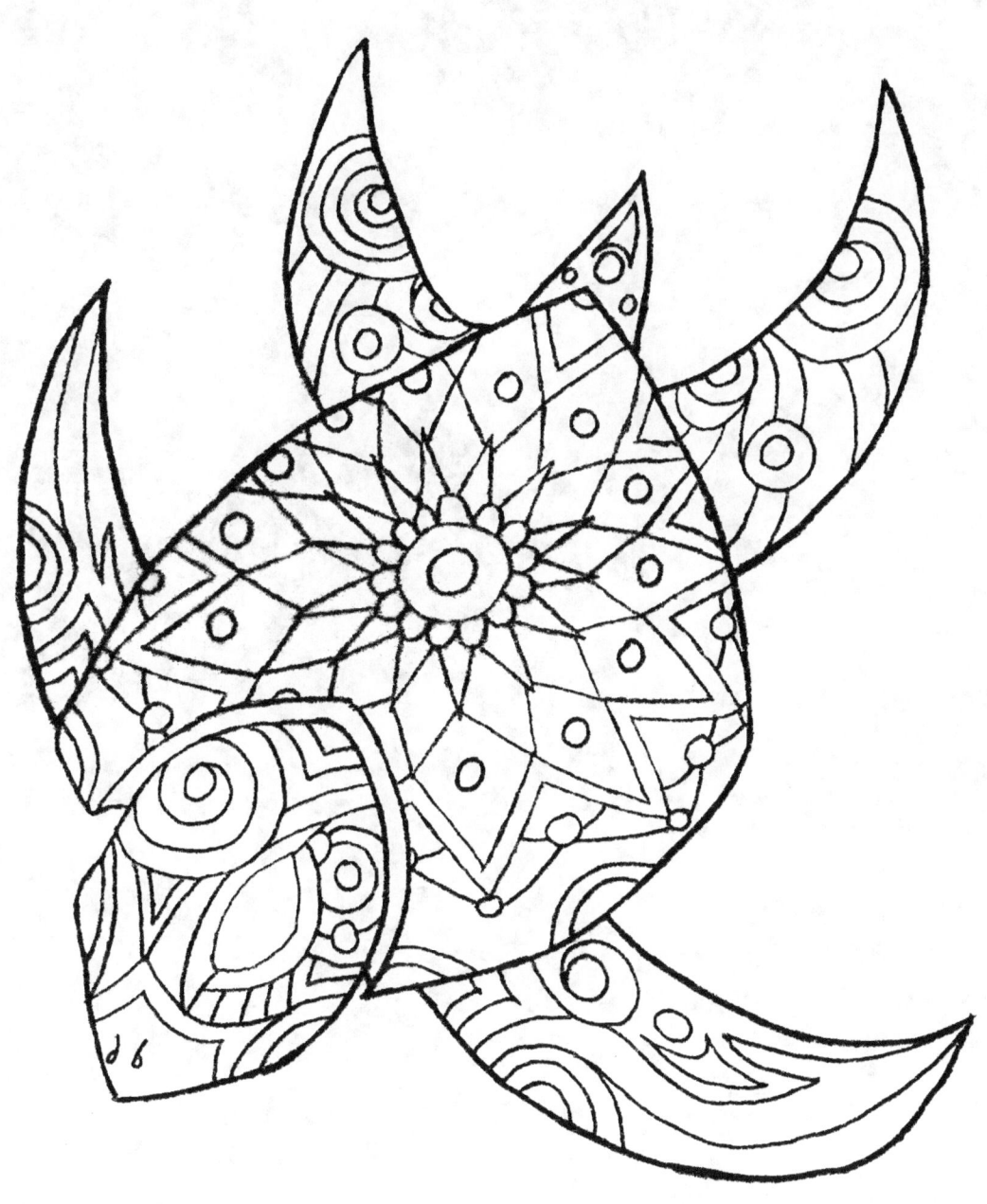

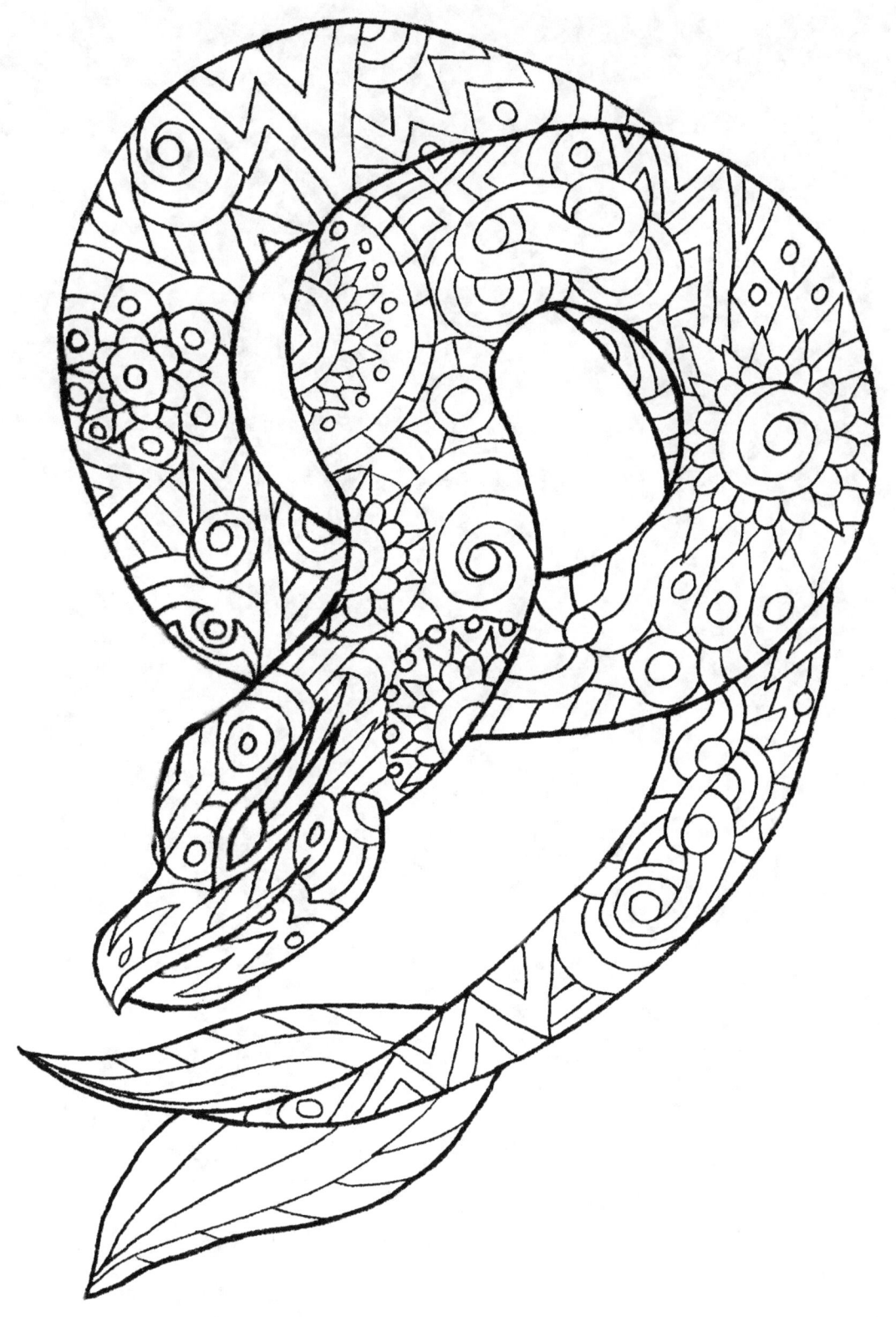

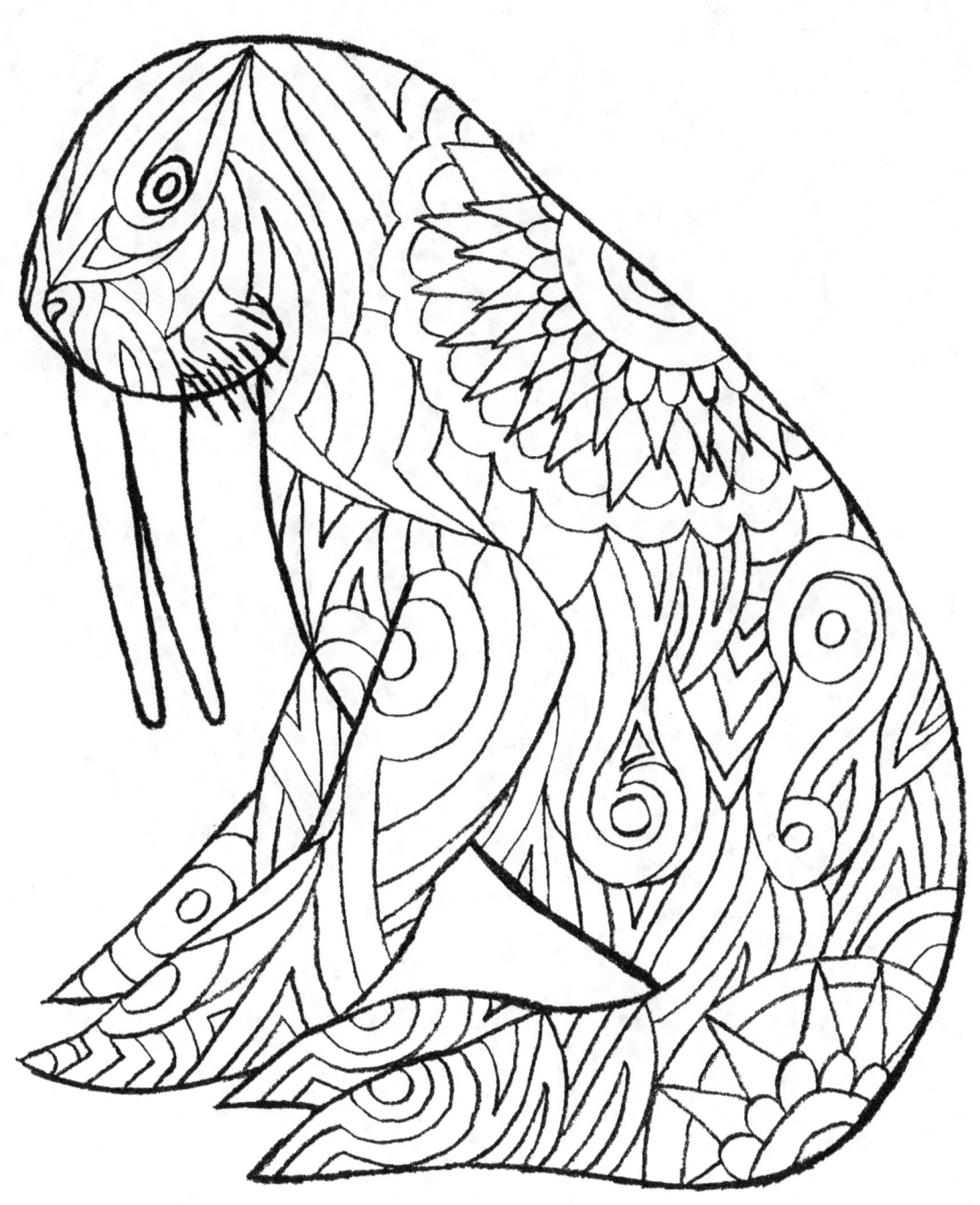

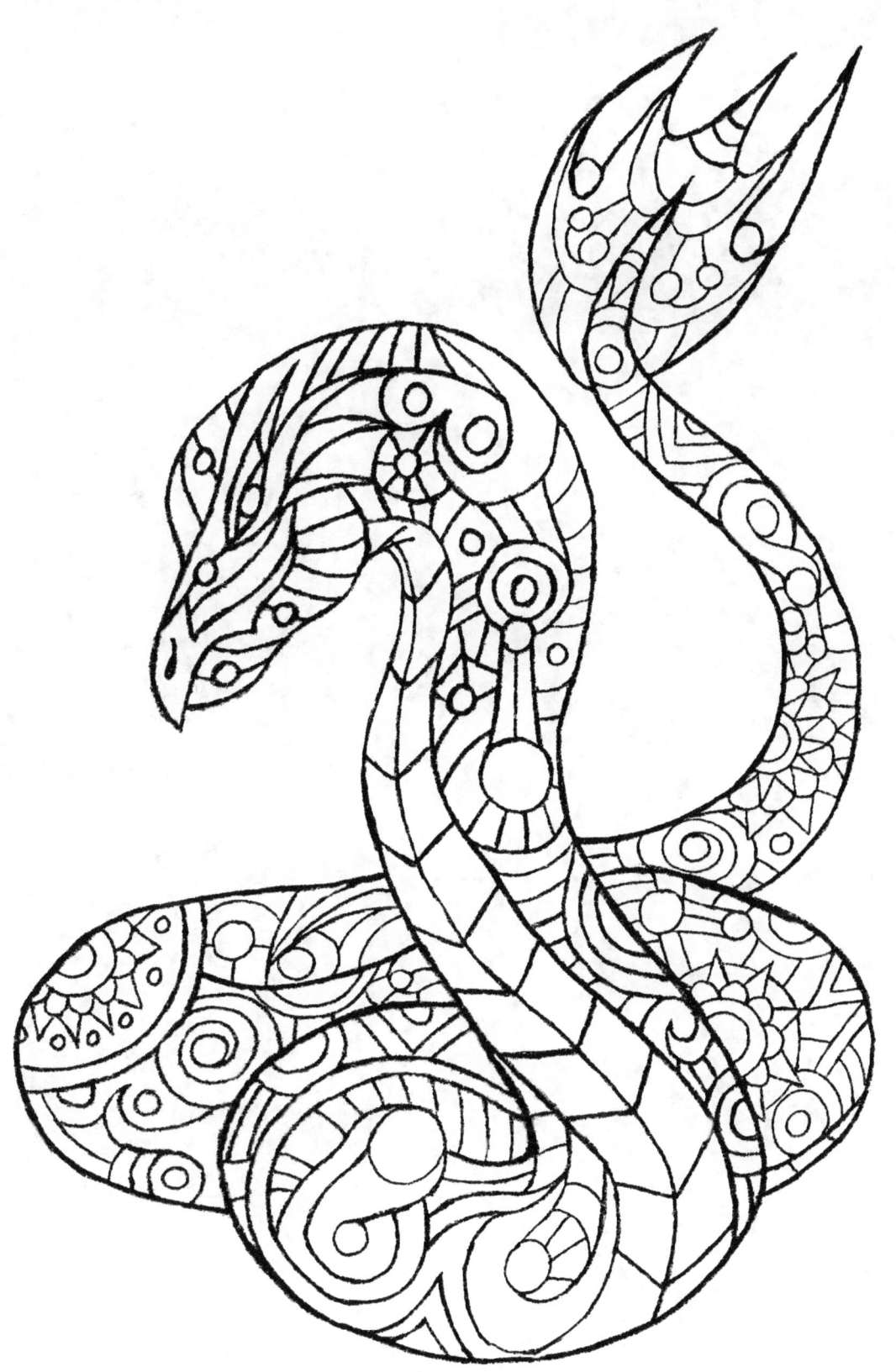

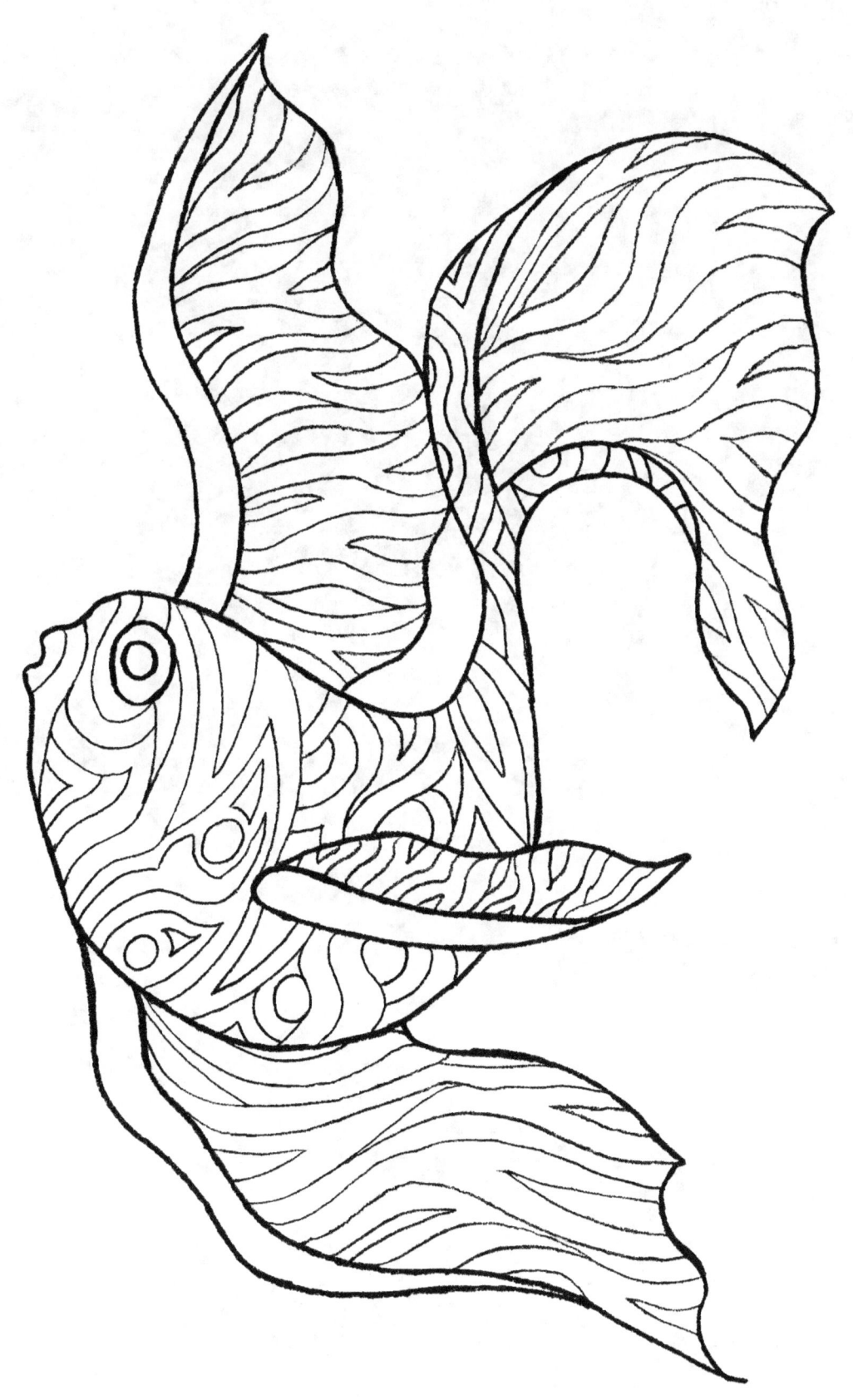

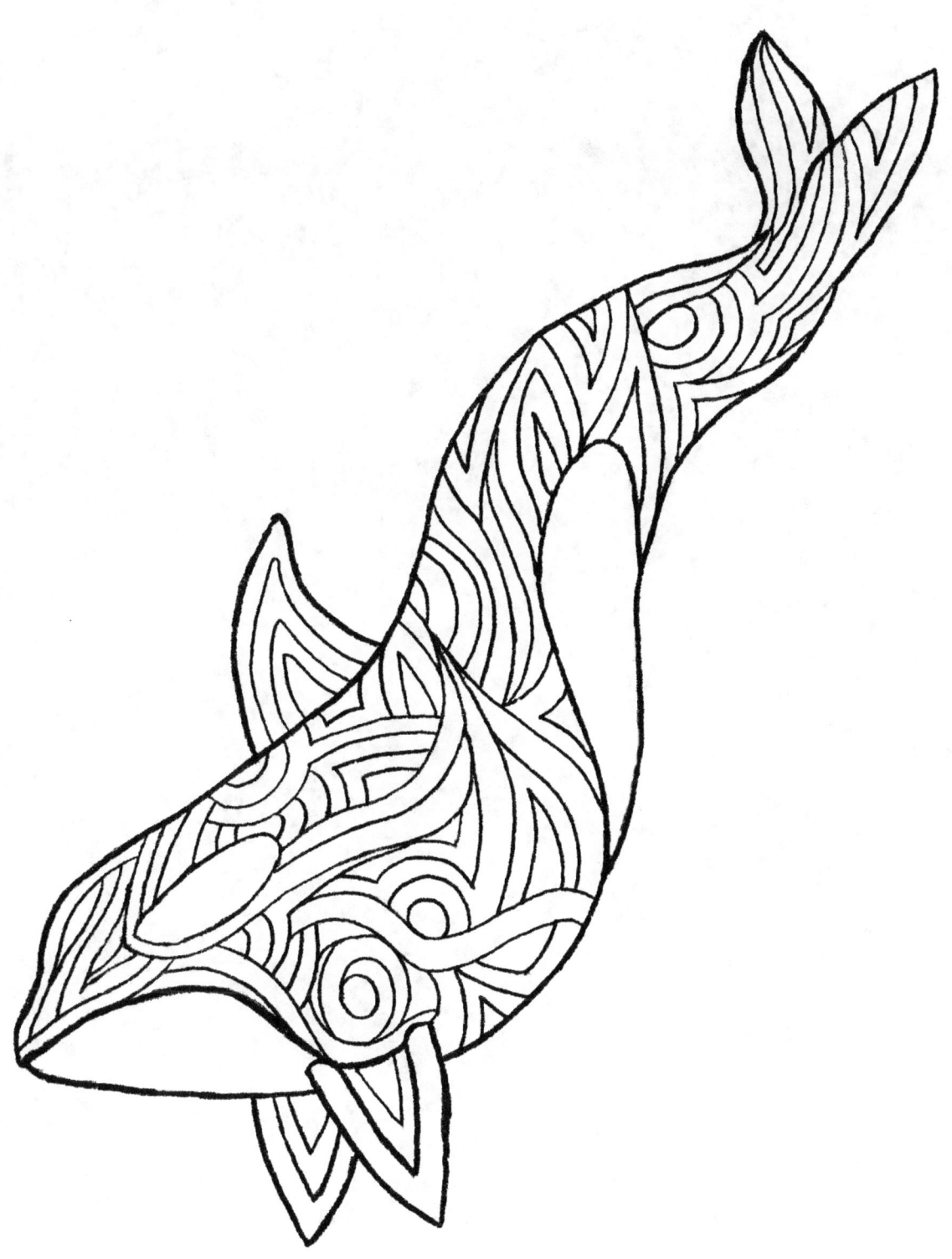

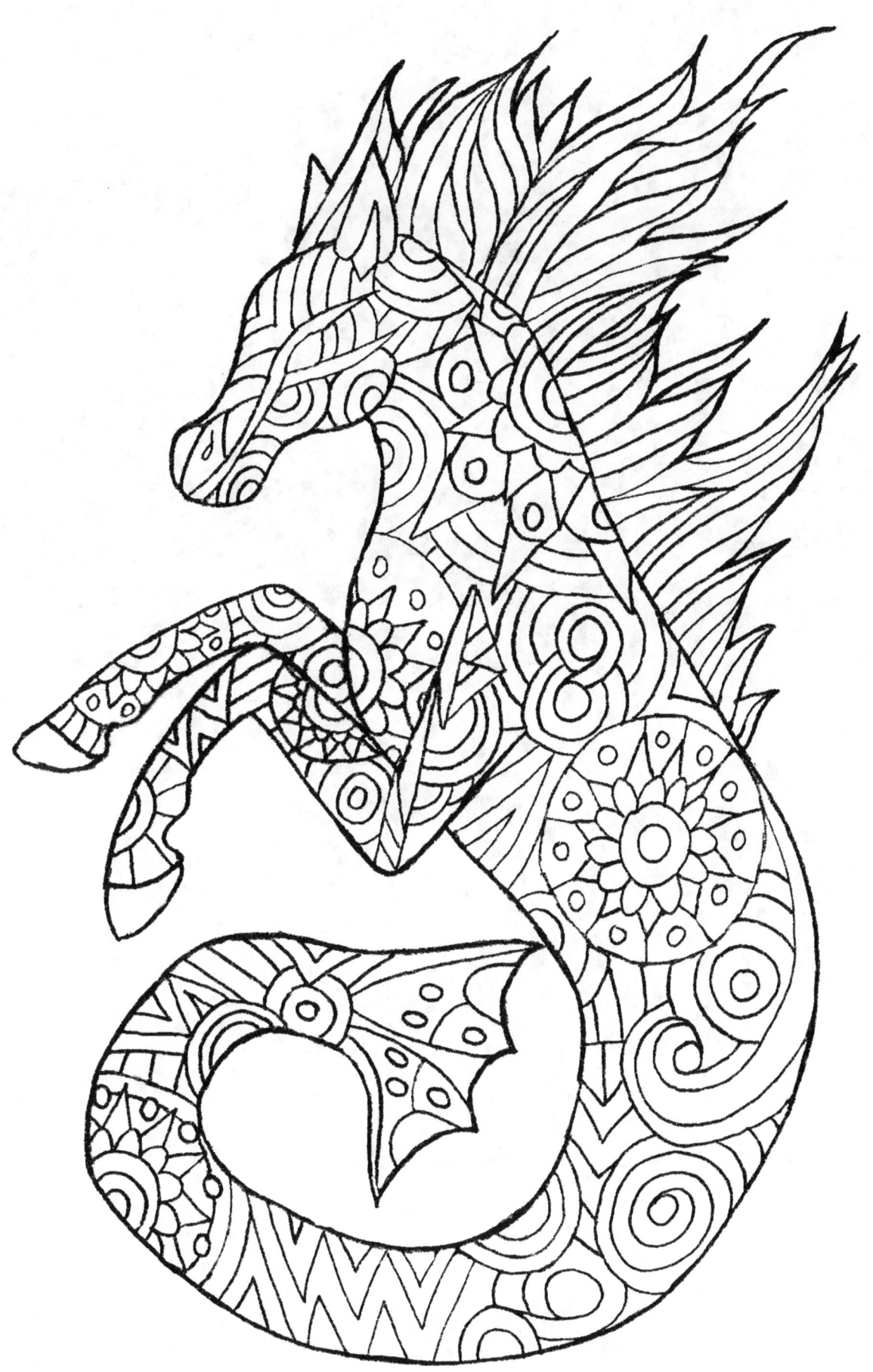

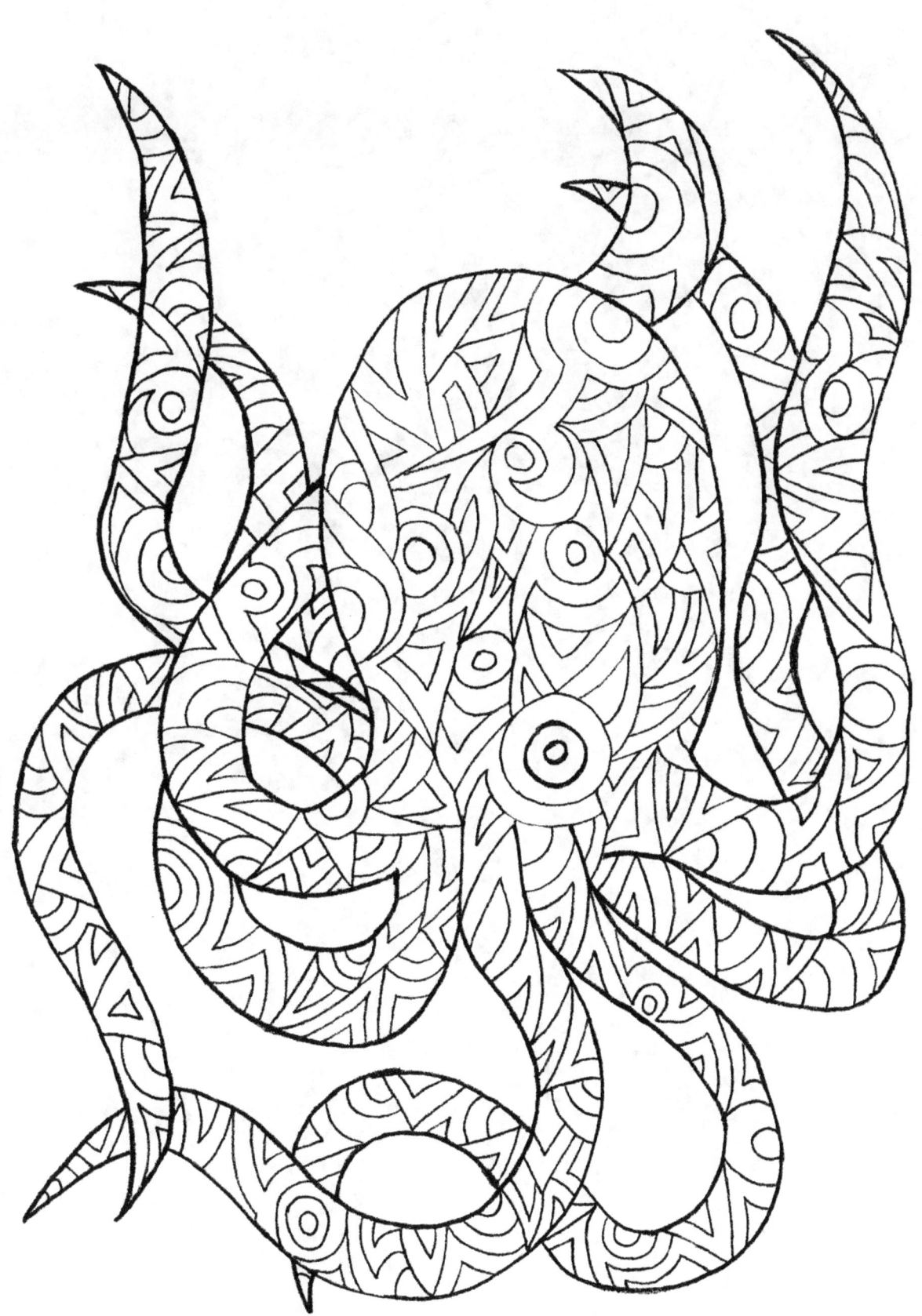

About the Illustrator

Josie has always enjoyed art in various forms and has written various stories. She found the design process of the coloring in images relaxing and stress relieving. She started the idea with a random image of a serpent (one which is found within this book) and filling it with designs and patterns. Realising many people may enjoy coloring in the images that began forming, she decided to publish them for all to enjoy. Having grown up with various friends and family suffering from depression, anxiety and other mental illnesses, she knows something so simple and basic can relieve our minds and free us even if only momentarily from our grinding and chaotic thoughts.

www.ingramcontent.com/pod-product-compliance
Lightning Source LLC
Chambersburg PA
CBHW081300180526
45170CB00007B/2511